HOLDING OUR BROKENNESS

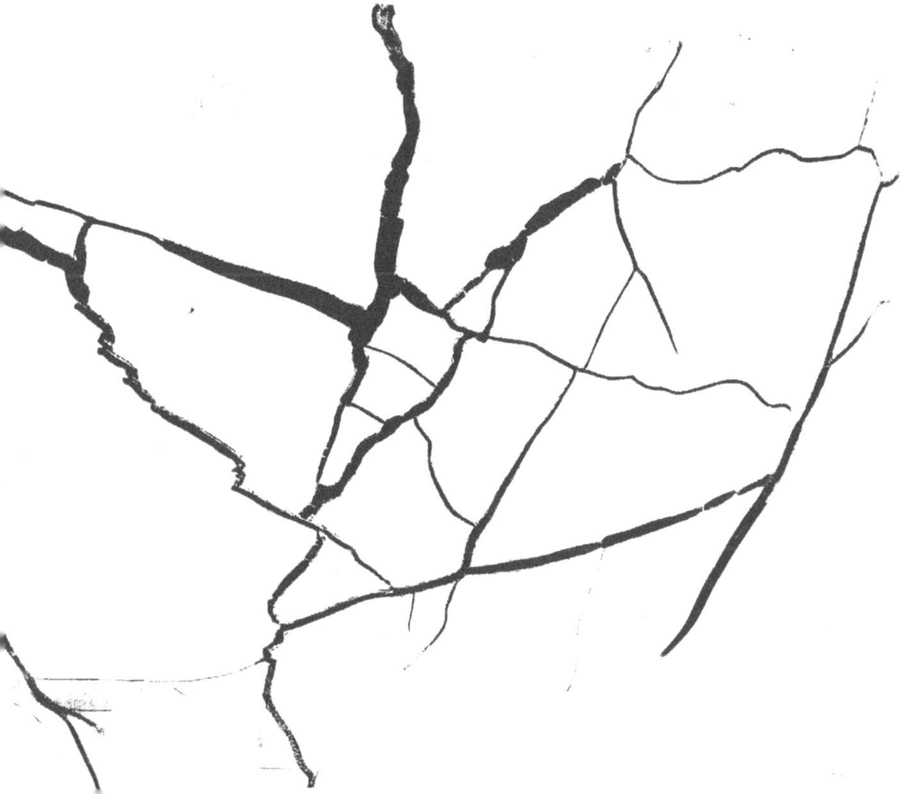

# Holding Our Brokenness

a gathering of poems:
twenty-five years

## Elizabeth Cunningham

BriarRose Books
New Paltz, New York

*Holding Our Brokenness: A Gathering of Poems: Twenty-five Years*
© Copyright 2025 by Elizabeth Cunningham

All rights reserved. No part of this book may be used or reproduced in any manner without the consent of the author, except in critical articles or reviews. Contact the author for information.

Paperback ISBN 978-1-944190-22-4

Cover photo by Ruth Cunningham
Book and cover design by Colin Rolfe
Briar Rose logo by David Budd

BriarRose Books
897 Briarwood Court
New Paltz, New York
https://elizabethcunninghamwrites.com/

# Contents

| | |
|---|---|
| preface | vii |
| one: my dark food and drink<br>from *Small Bird: poems and prayers* | 1 |
| two: the quiet place<br>from *Wild Mercy* | 9 |
| three: only the light remains<br>from *So Ecstasy Can Find You* | 20 |
| four: offering to the vanished god<br>from *Tell Me the Story Again* | 32 |
| five: not yet outgrown<br>from 2015 | 50 |
| six: threadbare<br>from 2016 | 55 |
| seven: vanished beauty<br>from 2017 | 60 |
| eight: who is playing that drum?<br>from 2018 | 71 |
| nine: beyond the world we see<br>from 2019 | 71 |

ten: a planet to adore                        79
from 2020

eleven: becoming where I am                   90
from 2021

twelve: coming in and going out              104
from 2022

thirteen: break us open not apart            108
from 2023

fourteen: a setting sun that will rise       113
from 2024

fifteen: companions on the way               129
from 2025

# Preface

A writer is one who writes. That much is clear. When someone asks what I write, my answer is novels. I seldom say "and poems." I used to admit to writing emergency poems, because they emerged, often out of a crisis. That is no longer true.

Writing poems has become a practice, often to avoid writing the next page or sentence of a novel-in-progress. Mostly because the practice of writing poems is a practice of noticing: the world outside and within, and the connections between the worlds. I am more apt to suspend judgment when I write poems. They don't have to work or advance a plot or make sense at all. They can be good or bad, and I know I won't know the difference for a while. So I let them be, returning to them, or not, to find out if they are complete or to complete them, if they are compostable or part of a harvest to share with others.

I hope the latter is true of the poems gathered here. I read poems as well as write them. And when a poem touches and gives voice to something in me I never/always knew was there, I save it. Poems can be personal and beyond personal at once, direct and oblique, particular and universal. What a form to attempt, what a field to play in, a wilderness where you can be both lost and found. And, one of my favorite places, a garden, where you can plant and tend and be constantly surprised by what comes up from the mystery of the ground.

The poems here have been gathered from twenty-five years of writing. My style has changed over time, particularly with regard to use of uppercase and punctuation. My intent is to be consistent within each poem. Please pardon my failures. The first four sections are selections from past collections, most out of print. The other

## preface

eleven sections are previously unpublished poems from 2015 to 2025.

Thank you for receiving them!

Special thanks to my laugh long, lifelong friend Cait Johnson for reading and rereading the poems and finding the perfect title.

—Elizabeth Cunningham

# my dark food and drink

from *Small Bird: poems and prayers*
published 2000 by Station Hill Press

## Heart Prayer

You can only pray what's in your heart

so if your heart is being ripped from your chest
pray the tearing

if your heart is full of bitterness
pray it to the last dreg

if your heart is a river gone wild
pray the torrent

or a lava flow scorching the mountain
pray the fire

pray the scream in your heart
the fanning bellows

pray the rage, the murder
and the mourning

pray your heart into the great quiet hands that can hold it
like the small bird it is.

## Prayer

O great mystery
take me to the deep place
where the root drinks dark water.
Take me to the ocean floor
where currents sway sea forests.
Show me the high places too
where the eagle rests on wind
and clouds tumble slowly
in their hugeness.
O mother father mystery,
I am a fretful child
flailing in my smallness.
Take me to your breast.
Let me ride the swells
of your slow, deep
breath

## Fall

We plop like fat acorns
or waft for miles on the wind
like milkweed seeds before
we light, but we fall, we fall
like the comet with its life-coded tail
like our fathers into our mothers
murky depths we fall
to this place this planet this
rock soil sea seedbed
where gods elbow each other
for a ringside seat to see us
break open and grow.

## Torch Singer

Forget what you see
the real me is wearing
a skimpy, sequined dress
overflowed by my breasts.
My finger and toe nails glitter
and I'm in a dive full of low light and life
and I'm singing.
My voice is dark
with something shining in it
like this scotch I'm drinking.

And when I sing
your sorrows flow into my song
like tributaries and I pay tribute
to them all.
When I sing my throat is huge
and blue as the sky.
I can hold the whole world
in one note
then let it fly.

## Sky

I love the sky
nothing else is big enough

I love how I forget it sometimes
take it for granted
like it was some big old ceiling
then it swoops down in a
grey swirl leaves spiraling
birds crossing to safety
winged boats to harbor.

I love how it draws me up
when I look
how sky blue can be brittle or soft
how it blooms in morning glories
in the last days before the first frost.

I love how the stars
dim and sharpen
how the moon rolls around
and around
losing and finding itself
in different quarters
different lights.

Somebody please
let me be a leaf
flying so high in the sky
I can't see myself
anymore.

## River Stick

I sit in a nest of tidal roots
under leaves lit by light on water,
their dapple changing
with ripple and wind.
A long curving stick rests lightly
in the same crux that cradles me.
Here take it, says the river.
Oh, no thank you (I am polite)
it looks so lovely where it is.
It is not as if it will stay here,
reasons the river, take it
to remember me by
the way I meander
the grain of my flow
the peace you know
when you're with me.

## What If

What if my heart is an opening rose
      and god is a honeybee gathering sweetness.

What if my mind is the crown of a tree
      and god is a wind raging there.

What if my soul is a deep root
      and god is my dark food and drink.

## Flower Light

At twilight I watch the black-eyed susans.
The grass and trees have gone grey,
the sky and river, grey,
but the susans hold their color.
I want to catch the moment
it disappears, so I do not
look at the lemon-wedge moon
or the first faint stars. I find
the yellow does not drift away
like a stick on the river
or scent on the air.
It dims slowly, seeping back
deep in the flower.

Then comes a moment
when the color brightens.
Maybe the moment when moonlight
overwhelms the afterglow,
the last moment of day,
the first moment of night.
The black-eyed susans shine from inside,
each petal shines,
and then their light goes out.

## The Old One Speaks

You must be unmade here
inside my grey cloak
inside my cold womb
here where the ice forms
and breaks
at the river's edge.

## Not Wasted

There are things I remember
like watching the stars come out
with my children when they were young.
How quiet and still we were.
The bats came out, too,
black and beautiful against
that transient sky—your couldn't
call it purple or blue—doing
their sonar dance with the bugs
while the birds gave a last twitter
or two. Sometimes the coracle moon
would be setting, the last light
lapping it silently.
We would watch together,
my children's mouths small
gaping nights and their eyes
that same dusk color
with the first stars floating in them.
And when I remember I know
I have not wasted my life.

## November Trees

In November when I see them
gathered grey, brown remnants
of leaf curling and wisping at their tips,
pooled in laps of roots, the trees
look like their own ghosts,
like lingering smoke, like incense
thick and sinuous. With the
green veil stripped away, I see
the whole trunk sways, as if
the trees are davening, these trees
who teach what temple columns are.

## Broken Home

Everything is here to stay,
one with the place we forgot to call home.
Shake the dust from your feet
and it remains the ground beneath them.
There is only change, river becoming rain
becoming river, fallen leaves
feeding the roots of trees feeding leaves.
It is the indestructible that destroys,
the things that won't break down
that may break us—unless
we break first, as an egg shatters
to release the bird
or a seed splits open and
takes hold in the earth.

# the quiet place

from *Wild Mercy*
published 2005 by Creatrix Resource Library, LLC

## Leaves

Everything I know about life and death
I learned from leaves
their iridescent youth
their dark tough serviceable summer
their brazen becoming of themselves
just before they let go
their Halloween afterlife
whispering  whispering.

## The Hanged One Reversed

The Hanged One reversed
is flying
rising.
She says
I am resurrection.
She says
all gravity turns to grace
as leaves to light.

She says
up and down don't matter anymore
inside and out
turn into each other.
She says
let go
fall fly.

## What Demeter Said

When my daughter went down
I took the sun
and hurled it against the hard sky
shattered it into a million shards
to seed the dark, to send down roots
to roof her world.

Surely, gods, that much is allowed
to scatter love blind into the mothering ground.

## Persephone's Turn

I never wanted to be Persephone
    (even though I was:
      booze and pills and blowjobs
      for strange men).
Who wants to rule the underworld with a rapist?

Let me spit out those seeds
    (let me spit it out).

I'm not going back.
You can't make me.

# What Kali Tells Me

It's all in the rhythm.
Falseness throws you off beat.
Rhythm renews your strength
with every step. That's how
time
becomes timelessness.

The trick is knowing
what needs to die
what is coming to birth.

All that clutter chokes
the next breath. Sillies,
by hoarding your toys
you stop the play.

Don't hold onto the tide.
Don't be a drag on the moon.
The wind is holding its breath
for you.

Let go let go let go.

## Riverboat

I take the wheel of the riverboat.
Aim for the cleft in the mountains,
the captain says. I keep turning
left, right, left, right
as the notch lists from my center.
You're over-steering, he says,
hold steady
let the boat come to rest.

## Breasts

Mountains are breasts
so are swells on the sea.
We live inside
a round blue breast of sky
milky with cloud.
Everywhere you look
the world is round.
Even when the sea is calm
even when there are no hills
you can see the curve.
The moon spills milk
all over everything.
The sun shines brightest
on breasts, always seeking
the heart in the hollow.
Everywhere we lay our heads on earth
that is her breast
that is her breast.

## As Dark

As dark as dirt
as dark as the dawn is cold
as dark as the drain
as dark as the earth is old

As dark as what I've longed for longest
as what I've lost and never found
as dark as what I hold the closest
as dark as an ear to the ground.

## Lost

When you are lost
pay attention to where you are.

Look for the slant of light
the way the stream runs
the shape of the slope
the moss on trees and rocks.

If the crumbs you scattered are gone
follow the birds.

## Night Rowing

Mist flows over the moon like water
moon on water lights the mist.
Let's take out the rowboat
in the chilly night over bath-warm water
thick with reeds that drape the oars
and loud with the rasp of lily pads over the keel.
Let's laugh till the night
hushes us with its hugeness
and we let go and drift with the mist
over and over the watery moon.

## Failed Gods

All parents are failed gods.
They do not keep the world safe.
They do not deliver happiness.

They throw their children out of Eden
to cover their own shame.

They grow old and frail.
Sometimes they are forgiven.

# Sacrifice

The gods will accept as sacrifice
whatever we bring to the altar
fears, shames, rages,
things we have hidden or denied.

The gods do not despise these gifts
the gift of what is wounded in us
the courage it takes to lay ourselves bare.

# The Quiet Place

I am slowly coming back
to the quiet place
the way a leaf eddies as it falls
the way a hush falls between waves
the way the wind falls at dusk.

## Moment

What is a moment?
When is it?
What is it made of?
How can you separate one
from another?

I am wondering
as I sit by the river
in a high, hot wind
that blows the river north
against the current.
I am wondering
as I smell the scent
the river leaves on the rocks.
I am wondering
as I look for patterns
in the grain of the driftwood
next to me.

Don't we have memories
that change meaning with the wheeling light?
Don't we have visions that draw us on
dark as a speck of bird in the shifting clouds?

If there is only this moment
where would the river be
the river's rise
the sea?

# The Hard Things

Paths of streams and lives
are formed by obstacles
things that cannot be moved
except by time or catastrophe
boulders, mountains, bone
of earth, the hard things
that happen to us, the hard things
we will not give up.

## Resurrection

Resurrection has nothing to do
with positive thinking.
It comes after ruin and surrender
surrender to ruin.
It comes after scorched or drowned earth
when the last hope dies
when everything dies
except the stubbornness of love.
Not defiant love, not
I love you anyway, so there.
Just that there's nothing else but love
even after you have lost faith
in its power. Still. Love.

That's when resurrection comes
not once but a thousand million times
with every death however small
every death that's complete
every death that closes over your head
with perfect blackness.

Only then
the miracle.

# Mercy's Face

There is a mercy in the tides
they come and go
they make new again
they bear no malice
towards the wreckage they toss or take.
If they are not mercy
they remind us of mercy.
They show us mercy's face.

# only the light remains

from *So Ecstasy Can Find You*
published 2015 by Hiraeth Press

## …it's enough

it is all poetry, even a dark morning
at the end of Fall, twisting oak branches revealed,
small birds and the last lacy leaves still holding fast

rivers and rivulets in the dirt after rain
also branch and curve like trees and hieroglyphic
trails of mice and birds and bees make more metaphor

a cloudy sky is only dull when you don't look
into all the layered meanings of grey and white
and catch the subtle motion of this dense, high mist

the rainbow rises and roots in forests of gold,
we the lucky ones who find the shining treasure
no need for pockets or sacks to carry it home

a white bird with wide wings flying from wood to field
huge and silent, not a hawk, could it be an owl?
everything in me quiets to watch and wonder

Elizabeth, what do you need to do but witness?
why do you trouble yourself with judging your worth?
climb the mountains, stand in your backyard, it's enough.

# Ecstasy

Ecstasy takes time, even if it lasts moments,
you have to slow down so ecstasy can find you
the way the light finds each plant in the sweep of a day
or the tide finds its secret way between dark rocks.
Stand still in the wood, on the shore, in your life.
Ecstasy will come, touch you, fill you, leave you changed.

## …or not

first take the sunlight inside your body and soul
then dip down into the darkness of the waters
add the salt of the earth, take a deep breath, you're here

from the middle of the pond I watch the moon wane
each day thinner and thinner, higher and higher
she's fading into light, revealing her dark face

buzzards high above fly a silent circle song
the cicada's drone draws out the end of summer
my heart swings wide, wild, child on a carnival ride

I am old and older, adrift in my last days
I am a child, standing on a rock by a lake
I am neither, only the whirl of wind, light, wave

over and over I witness the round from shoot
to bud to flower to seed or seed within fruit
always a fall, the dying back down to the root

I look for metaphors, I seek to know my phase
fresh, fading, bearing fruit or rot, Elizabeth,
life will rise again, whether it is yours—or not.

# Picking blackberries

Back in Eden under
the power lines we move
through the bramble thicket
beckoned on and on
by the blackest berries.
The birds cry out their
protest at our intrusion
but as we deepen
into rhythm of this ancient
bliss, the birds go back
to singing. Abundance.

## ...bear witness back, be here

frost in the night, shining at dawn, melting at noon
flowers give up the ghost on black funeral stalks
I come with the clippers and cart away my dead

light shining through windows and cracks in the old barn
makes patterns with the beams, the weathered boards, the dust,
draws my attention, turns me to some mystery's heart

the tender of an empty shrine, that's what I am
the gods may be here, though the devotees have gone
still, the sleeping ground is alive, birds feast on seeds

hawks roll over on the wind as if on a bed
big spruce lies on the lawn, a dogwood crushed beneath
in the same storm's wake, downed trees, playful birds of prey

some are planters, some tenders, others harvesters
of a field, a time, a place. After the fall falls
who watches, sings, and sweeps until it's time to sleep

Elizabeth, the land is your wordless witness
forms pass, trees and buildings fall, people come and go
stop trying to stop them, bear witness back, be here.

## Hard frost

this morning the frost
in the fallen leaves shines,
the morning glories sag
on the vine, their ghost
given up to the blue sky

# Heart: after the Lord's Prayer

O broken heart
here in this broken world
your truth be told
your healing be one
with the healing of this earth
that is our heaven.
In you we have everything we need.
We forgive ourselves and everyone else.
In your daring we are safe.
For you are our strength and our grace and our home
now and beyond time.

# Beware

beware anyone who demands or expects you
to submit to his or her will
even god doesn't do that
especially god doesn't do that

## ...only the light remains

When the tide turns, between one breath and another
what gathers in this empty place where power rests?
My life pauses here unknown to itself and me.

The one I believed in is called the way. Is he
a deer thicket, a swarm of bees, my bravery
as I prepare for undress rehearsal of death?

Whoever you are do not put us to the test
we are bound to fail, deliver us from the hook
the one you baited and dangled, the one we took.

Learn to angle yourself to the wind, to the wave,
you are your own vessel, you wield the paddle's blade,
a slight turn and struggle yields to the flow of grace.

Don't you know monarchs can fly over continents
antennae mapping the mother wind, feet sensing
nectar miles below, telling them when to let go?

Sometimes you don't see the bird, only the shadow,
winged darkness sweeping over the ground or your face,
you look up, it's too late, only the light remains.

## haiku

don't dim your joy
you might be a distant star
in someone's dark night

## ... listening to the ground

no objective correlative for this hard time
more life in a desert than in desolation
this grief is punctuation. stop. what can be next?

the pressure of sorrow and terror, internal,
external, what is being ground to dust between
these real or imagined huge and relentless stones

outside the window above the altar, a rock
cliff more ancient than the church, crevices alive
with moss and fern, rising to bare sentinel trees

there is never just one death, each person's dying
takes so much with it, the form of a family
and other circles that held her, that she helped hold

the ducks and geese know where they are going and why
they splash land, they lift off and fly, ripples remain
till they widen out and out into the unseen

Elizabeth, it is more than your friend you miss
stay here with yourself awhile, be patient, be still
while you grieve your feet are listening to the ground.

## haiku

in the end we're bared
leaves, lives stripped to branch and bone
who abandoned us?

two small carved pumpkins
side by side on the grey rock
their aging faces

## Parting of the long-married

He opens the car door
and begins to get in
before I protest and he
swears he would have remembered
to give me a goodbye embrace.

He insists on removing my glasses
to hold me close, and I (almost angrily)
say many useless things
about calling and staying safe.
I send a blessing as he drives away.

Later I cannot find my glasses.
It is clearly his fault.
I rewind the morning and know
I put them on the back of the car.
I find them halfway up the drive, unharmed.

# Saints' gold

the light shining
through your mother's womb
the light shining
into the depths of the sea
the last light on the last
oak leaves
at the end of a short
November day
the honey inside the hive
the honey spooled
on the spoon
the light in your lover's
eyes when he knows
you will never
leave

## My Life as a Fish

When my mother was the ocean
I was a fish. I loved to swim in her.
She was warm and vast. Sometimes
light filtered through her fathoms
and I swam deep in her brightness.

At last I grew larger than the largest
whale. I pressed against her shores,
her rocks and found my way
through a narrow cave
into the ocean of air.

Now whenever I swim
my spine remembers being a fish
Whenever I swim
I bless my mother and swim
in the memory of her.

## the last dance

it will be all right
when it comes,
the last dance, the one
I've waited for all my life

no matter the manner
of my struggle,
long pain or sudden ending,
there will come the tap

on my shoulder
as death cuts in on life
and I, no follower,
will follow this last partner

death's sure hands will
guide me, spin me, invite
my hips to rock and
snake my liquid limbs

before I take
whatever form or
formlessness is next
death will unfurl

the impossible beauty
of my body and grant me
grace, my grace, eternal,
gone before I know

# offering to the vanished god

from *Tell Me the Story Again*
published 2019 by Epigraph Books

## scribe song

the scribe waits under the oak
watching the last leaves fall
some red, some rust, some
holding the green edge of fire

*these are the leaves*
*these are the leaves*
*of the ancient book*
*the story is ending*
*tell me the story again*

the scribe waits for the river
or mountain, the small brave mouse
or shadowing raven, ready
to write the translation

*these are the wings*
*these are the feet*
*of the unwritten book*
*the story's beginning*
*tell me the story again*

the scribe waits, scrapes
the flesh of her story
down to the bone, her own
blood will do for ink

*this is the bone*
*this is the blood*
*of the book she is writing*
*the story still spinning*
*tell me the story again*

offering to the vanished god

## song to mother rain

mother rain, come down,
wrap us in your grey shawl
round and round and round.
touch the tender life
deep, deep underground
sweet mother rain, come down.

## sorrow singer's grave lament

and where shall we honor our dead
who are not ours anymore, now we
have left them, wandered from shore
to shore, followed water
to its hidden source to hide
in mists made of remorse?
oh, the wide plain in the sun, gone, gone.
oh, the labors, the loving, the feasting, done.

the dead are still our own,
the whole earth holds them,
our grave, too, our bed, our bone.
no, we have not left our dead,
there is nowhere to go but home.

# temple sweeper's song

they say the gods are gone from here,
they said the gods are ghosts,
dead as their devotees, but I remain
unsheltered from sun, from rain
in a roofless ruin where wildflowers
succor the last wild bees.
there is pollen and leaf and snow.
the gods still dance in motes of dust
I stir and sweep day after day,
believing still in the slightest chance
someone will come from far away, from long ago
to sweep me into the dance.
by firelight our shadows will leap
and the gods will reappear.

offering to the vanished god

## sword woman's song

wear your life lightly
like the garment it is, don't
clutch it to you tightly,
let it ride the wind.
sword woman, you say, where
is your armor, where is your shield?
beloved, my armor is to yield.
I fear no cliff edge.
I fly from tree to tree
landing softly on a limb,
death to one side, life
to the other, I love both
and fear neither, there is no strife,
no shield but flashing sword
bright in the sun. if you kill me
I love you still, the same
if I kill you.

## stone mountain song

how can you hear my voice?
you come to me for silence
for wind in the pines
for water running underground
for the slow wheeling of vultures
over my bare height
for blue sky beyond shadow
in the strong hot light.

it was not always so.
loud rang the hammer and chisel
as I was taken piece by piece
to be millstone or city,
stripped of trees, a barren place
where only berries grew, you
stole those too, took them to your tables
miles and rivers below.

now I have taken back
mist and tree, moss and fern
and mystery. bears and snakes sleep
deep in hidden winter warmth
and wild cats roam. stay. I will
chide no more, small one,
forgotten, forgetting, alone.
cling to me now, I will be your home.

offering to the vanished god

## ancient dreamer's song

you don't need open eyes to see,
you don't need to be awake to wander.
the mountain thinks it's old
but I am older. if you see me,
and maybe you won't, don't
tread on my mossy bed, don't disturb
my fine-woven cloak, fresh flowers,
fallen leaves, don't disturb my powers,
bound and freed by dreams.

## song of the merry drunk

I distill dew from the grass
rain from the leaves
birdsong from the breeze.
all berries are mine in their season,
wine for as long as it lasts.

vote with your feet, vote with your feet,
I sing with the redwing.
eat your peas, eat your peas,
is what poor will is really saying.
I sing with the songbirds, grok with the ravens.

no barstools here, pull up a rock.
tell me your troubles, whoever you are..
mine are all drowned, down the stream,
down my throat, so I sing you a song
all on one note, la la la, la la la, la la la, la.

come, sing with me. drowned sorrows
all flow to the sea, the faraway sea
where raucous seagulls sing off key.
the ground is soft and my snoring sweet.
no need to tiptoe, I'll sleep, then I'll drink.

## storm singer

look! can you see it there
in the empty air,
whirling in the swirl of my palm?
you think, too small,
a storm is big! really,
there is not much difference at all.
listen! the storm is singing for you,
your rage, your grief,
your ecstasy unleashed.
the storm is singing to the earth,
the earth is singing to herself
and I am the keeper of the song.
I hold it in my hand,
I fold it into my heart.
don't fear the storms, fearful one,
there is no intent to harm,
a broken world must breathe.

## morose fool's song

no one is laughing,
I was never funny.
there was no king, nor queen neither
to amuse or call to account for their sins
against the people, their sins
against owl and fish and wolf
against water and wind and honest work.
the powerful hide behind
the fools they thrust out front,
the ones they let us believe we chose.
the fools are us.
the bells on my cap don't jingle,
nor yet the bells on my toes.
I don't know how to cut a caper
or prophesy the doom already come.
do you notice? I can't even rhyme.

offering to the vanished god

## great oak song

hush now, small one.
I have not spoken yet, though I have grown
in silent rings three hundred years,
though I groan in wind that gives me
voice as light gives me
new limbs and earth opens to me
its depths where my roots taste truth
in rock and water.
come into the shelter of me
and lay down your despair,
come into the shelter of me
and be silent,
come into the shelter of me
and remember
you are a child among elders.
small one, you've forgotten your task
small one, you're forgiven before you ask.

## temple sweeper remembers

when the summer wind blows a certain way,
a few yellow leaves fly,
falling though it is not fall.
there is a sadness no different
from happiness and a happiness
holding sadness, same as the summer
wind holds those leaves in the air
as long as it can. then I remember the long-ago.
I remember something I called
love and maybe it was.
if I lean on my broom a certain way,
I will almost—but never quite—fall.
there is a yellow leaf on a broken stone,
the wind's offering to the vanished god.

## song to the ancient dreamer

your face a dry leaf,
your bone made of stone.
ancient dreamer, take me down
to what you know.

*unknown, unknown*
*hear the wind moan*
*what I know cannot be known*
*only dreamed, only dreamed.*

your hands trailing tendrils,
your feet made of moss,
ancient dreamer, lead me on
to what you know.

*unknown, unknown*
*a knife edge to be honed,*
*what I know cannot be known*
*only dreamed, only dreamed.*

your mouth a hollow,
you belly a mound,
ancient dreamer, take me in
to what you know.

*unknown, unknown*
*all life is on loan.*
*what I know cannot be known*
*only dreamed, only dreamed.*

## sorrow singer's respite

when I cast my sorrow down,
I see shattered pieces on the rocks
catching light, jewel-like, sea glass,
some shards smooth, some jagged.
I hear laughter, foolish, high,
a seagull's cry. it is my voice, my voice.
what's happened to my song?

did I dash my sorrow on these rocks?
is there something succulent inside?
I only know I am rising into the air
willy-nilly against my will.
I don't know how to get back down.
where is my gravity?

you have done you worst, life,
here is my life,
this strange pattern glittering below.
you have done your worst, life,
here are our lives—and deaths
and desperations,
our craven and courageous acts,
our loves lost and tossed to the wind
to fall again, here, there,
beautiful, scattered, here, there
beautiful, gathered.

I touch ground again.
I take up my burden, it is light.
I sing my sorrow, it is sweet.

offering to the vanished god

## temple sweeper wonders

can any task lead to god?
picking fleas off a cat,
sweeping up the mouse droppings
once again, doing whatever you must do
even if you are afraid,
even if you recoil?
doing it till the fear and revulsion
go away or you can't feel them anymore.
the sun keeps rising and setting,
the stars keep wheeling,
the moon disappears and appears.
beauty is relentless,
even if it doesn't feed you
or keep you warm.
one moment I think,
good, I've almost made it through.
the next, oh no! it's almost gone.
I sweep the floor again.
I wonder what else I am supposed to do.
god come find me, god become me,
a seeker with a broom.

## the man who does not speak watches the ancient dreamer sleep

her hands move like sea fronds,
slowly up and down on some current
I cannot see. where has she gone?
where does she go? can I go, too,
beyond, between, to a place
where memory doesn't matter anymore?
her words are slipping down a stream,
yellow leaves, fallen, forgotten, their
green life only a dream.

## the scribe's task

when rivers carry mountains to the strand,
she must stand midstream to catch the muddy
gold in her hand, and when she sees the sea rise
to meet the land, she must remember,
every story holds the power to surprise.

offering to the vanished god

## ancient dreamer awakes

I dreamed I was a tall tree,
mightier than most.
I gave shelter to many.
my shadow was very long,
like my almost eternal life.

now I wake to an empty sky.
when the mighty fall,
the world must shift.
what will grow, I wonder,
in all the light I've left?

## the silence of the stones

we will have the last word,
we will have the last silence.
even if the earth quakes,
even if the water
wears us away
and away.
still we have seen it all.
we bear witness
to all folly and bravery,
to all struggle, all defeat.
but we won't speak those words.
we don't judge,
we render silence.
beautiful bones, one day you will all be
beautiful bones,
like us.

## ancient dreamer dreams on

the mountain thinks it's old,
but I am older.
I am stars and dust and ocean.
I am the lap
that will hold you all
in the end, beyond the end.
oh, my children, my wilted flowers,
my fallen trees and heroes,
my scrabbling, swimming creatures,
my crying, flying winged ones,
come home, come home
all is lost and never lost.
come home to me,
come home.

# not yet outgrown

## from 2015

### image

Moses, Jesus, Buddha, Mohammed,
the more or less historical avatars,
sitting at a table, maybe playing cards
or counting up poker chips. how many
have killed for your religion?
how many have died? are the founders
gleeful or depressed, exalted or ashamed?

### another image

and sitting nearby on boulders
next to a whitewater creek
the wrathful and merciful goddesses,
considering destruction and succor.
now and then, they dance on stones
in the stream, the ancient, always new
dance of death and birth, rising
and receding. what will become
of our darling, devastated planet?
they are not sure yet,
they are not worried.

## now and then, plants and men

I used to be attracted to men
now I prefer plants
(so much more varied and pleasing)

I used to want men to admire me
now I am content to admire leaf and flower
(so varied and so pleasing)

I like it when the red oak
waves her leaves at me
I believe my love is fully requited

I could never tell with men

## summer solstice tree villanelle

the great old oak tree will gather me in
when earth shifts its tilt to gathering night
and three hundred spiraling circles spin

I call out the woman and child I've been
the child at play, the mother full of might
the great old oak tree will gather us in

the deep noon silence stills the human din
all that I am floats to the tree's great height
and three hundred spiraling circles spin

drawn to the core by the deep-rooted yin
I yield my eyes to arboreal sight
the great old oak tree has gathered me in

see the acorn, the whole tree held within
falling to earth through ancient autumn light
till three hundred spiraling circles spin

when waxing light ends, waning must begin
fathoms underground the first root holds tight
to my core I've gathered my old selves in
and numberless spiraling circles spin

## well-dressed

I wish I could wear a river
the flow and fall of water
how it curves against rock
makes light into colors no one can name

I wish I could wear moss
and lichen, grow my clothes
like a rock or a fallen tree
and who would not want to sport ferns?

and why not wear a low meadow mist
or a sweep of cloud. earth is always
so well dressed and, even bared,
there is the elegance of roll and dip and shadow.

## elk dream

before dawn, between night and day,
between sleeping and waking,
I roll on my side and then
I am standing at the edge of the field,
four-legged and massive, antlered.
I run, my legs coming down
in a quadruple rhythm the ground gives back,
turning my weight to springing grace.
I run on, a warm-blooded ship,
over swells of earth, light, heavy,
free of doubt, back into dream.

## ambition

I want to be a river never doubting its flow
or a wind that pauses now and then to listen
to silence, a seed sown, a life not yet outgrown.

# threadbare

published 2016

## do bodies wear out like clothes

I love my threadbare clothes
their softness, skin showing through the holes
garments only to be worn at home.
even mended, it's only a matter of time
before they fall away or have to be let go

will I wear my body like that
love it worn and frail
colors faded, shape lost
but so soft, so familiar
home, home
only a matter of time
before it falls away
before it asks to be let go.

## between future and past

my children will grow
into a future I will never know

just like the present I inhabit
for so many people in the past

how can they be gone
my parents, grandparents, mother-in-law?

and gone, too, the overfull middle of my life
when I was linchpin between the generations

this past still swirls around my ankles,
a wave receding, ebbtide

the sand sucked away under my feet
someday the wave of the future will knock me down

## be still

be still and if you never know god
you will hear the hummingbird sip nectar
from the hosta and watch the determined
toil of an ant in the vast world next
to your feet, you will mark the premature
fall of a hickory nut, across the field
a raven will open her throat and send
her wild resonance to your ear, all the birds
will forget you are there and go back to
bobbing and weaving, earth to branch to air

## dream

we find saint Sarah
made of mounds of river stone
blue loose-woven dress,
carbon dated, eons old
help me remember her song

## noon villanelle

I have come to love the silence of noon
the cars have all gone wherever they go
I can hear the bees buzz their tuneless tune

the noon of the day is the sun's full moon
listen, the air is still, the wind lies low
I have come to love the silence of noon

the chainsaws silent, no wood to be hewn
no scratching the dirt, it's too hot to hoe
I can hear the bees hum their tuneless tune

each shadow cast, now drawn close, is a rune
thickets conceal spotted fawns and a doe
I have come to love the silence of noon

this refuge from noise, a sweet daily boon
a full body blessing, crown to tiptoe
I can hear the bees buzz their tuneless tune

each noon is a moment, passing so soon
the wild meadow flowers before we mow
I have come to love the silence of noon
I can hear the bees hum their tuneless tune

threadbare

## dream

green latrine, green death
I am in line for which one?
both involve a hole

# miracles

the root of the word is *mirari*: to wonder
maybe *mira!* in Spanish shares the root

look! sometimes all it takes is
walking in a different direction

on the route you usually take,
the familiar revealed as wonder-full

being present at the moment the ice
begins to form on the stream

silvering the rocks beneath the green
flow, creeping out over the still places

or glimpsing the eyes of a lost child
in someone you fear or hate, even if you

can't reach him or her, just knowing—
deep in recesses of flesh, hollow of bone

there is innocence. I admit things look bad now
wars, repressions, persecutions, extinctions

flood, fire, climate changing beyond our ken
still, miracles are scattered like frost crystals

in cold winter light, small kindnesses everywhere,
and now and then a joke on us that we all get.

# vanished beauty

from 2017

## house plants

when I was outside
I saw my houseplants
peeking out the window
the one with red-tongue leaves
and the pale white narcissi.
sure, they are sun-seeking yet
how curious they appear
as if they are fascinated
by those big plants, the trees,
where birds perch and
squirrels climb and leap.
my oxalis is old and wise
has spent whole summers
outside. I can tell you
what rain feels like,
s/he tells the others, and wind
moving in your leaves.
you have to hope you don't
attract bugs and deer
but it is good to be outside.
the sun can be fierce
but the shade in the afternoon
is deep and sweet.
the trees watch over us
and for a while we are wild.

## our last hours

the birds sing for us
my hand lightly touches you
we are together

## …his vanished beauty

grief really is heavy, its weight no mere cliché
a weight bending the bough with yearning for the ground
those layers of soil and rock and rain fallen down

on the top rung of a ladder, head tilted back
I attempt to prune the deathless wisteria
bare branches a golden tangle against blue sky

I can tell I'm upset; I'm counting syllables
tanka, haiku, ghazal, maybe a villanelle
no freeform wail, only mourning in strict measure

in the sudden cold a few confused peepers peep,
aggrieved and mournful, what happened to the party?
yesterday spring was in full swing, now, what the fuck!

small birds everywhere undaunted by the weather
each wing stroke a strobe shadow on the sunny road
they're the things with feathers, hope is superfluous

he bequeathed to me the tiny sheaths of his claws
left in the carpets he was not supposed to scratch
I cherish these remnants of his vanished beauty

## resurrection

the Christians got it right
new life out of death and ruin

but who showed them
this good news?

the earth
the earth

## canvassing for voter registration on Downs Street

Three men, white, brown, black,
changing a flat tire.
People in green hats and beads
coming and going
from the St Patrick's Day parade.
An old woman on the walk
outside her house,
"You're too late! I'm too old!
I did all this shit before!
My bags are packed for Canada!"
The man with teeth almost worn away
and a diabetic infection in his foot
that won't heal. The black woman
who invites us in from the cold
and says, "Yes, I'll be there next Tuesday!"
A kindly Irish-American man with artificial
flower arrangements all over his porch
whose kids are at the parade.
A Hispanic man who says proudly,
"I am registered, democratic."
An old black man on his steps
who explains he is smoking tobacco
not weed! "I gave that up," he says.
He says he doesn't do too well
with reading mail, but wants
the voter registration form
to fill out maybe later.
A Hispanic man visiting a friend

*vanished beauty*

who speaks Spanish only.
He invites us to go in with him
and translates for us.
"Terrible things are happening," he says.
Then he looks at us and smiles,
"But we are not alone, thank you
for coming out in the cold, thank you."

## dream

she shouts for Jesus,
the dying nun in my arms,
what takes him so long?
I wrap her in a blue robe
she dies humming a soft song

## effortless

maybe prayer can be effortless
not even as forceful as a light breeze
more like a current of air,
the prayer caught up and carried
bright and silent as a seed

## ravens

for once there are no humans climbing the crag,
their silly talk bouncing from rock through unimpeded air.
instead seven ravens sit or flit from rock to rock,
their voices made for sky and stone and tree top.
one calls and calls, two converse, some are silent.
several lift their wings and hold them to the light.
I watch them from far below, under leaf cover.
if they know I am there, they have no reason to care.
the white rock, the wind-bent pines, the blue sky, all theirs.

## the coming of the rain villanelle

I love to watch the coming of the rain
the stillness just before the wind lets go
erratic turning of the weather vane

the tall trees shake their branches like a mane
loosing leaves and birds in a swirling flow
I love to watch the coming of the rain

the sky is covered with a purple stain
the air is lurid with a greenish glow
erratic turning of the weather vane

between the storm and me no window pane
when the first drops touch the leaves I will know
I love to watch the coming of the rain

sometimes it seems the world has gone insane
the news each day can strike us like a blow
erratic turning of the weather vane

rain, soak the ground and wash away our pain
we know you fall alike on friend and foe
I love to watch the coming of the rain
erratic turning of the weather vane

# woodchuck

at last, at summer's last gasp,
my husband has trapped
a persistent woodchuck
in a have-a-heart trap.
he feeds him tomatoes
and plans to take him
to freedom—and exile—
the next morning
but he forgets till afternoon.
I watch him carry the trap
to the car. The woodchuck's nose
is bloody with attempted escape.
he is fierce and alive. when he
looks at me, I feel a shock of kinship
creature to creature, life to life,
alive, trapped, determined
we are the same animal,
we are the same.

## virginity

I wish I had enjoyed mine
not thought of it as uncool
an embarrassment to be disposed of
as soon as possible
without ceremony

I wish I had prized mine
not for any moral reason
not because anyone said
it must be kept till marriage
but because it was mine

I miss/ed my wild young power
the swelling bud that holds
all mystery, all possibility. once
that moment, perfect,
unnoticed, was mine

## oak shine

the oaks have not loosed all their leaves
they are brown, they are brittle, they shine
even the ones fallen on my path
are bright with the late sun's light
if I keep walking along this oak-lit path
I might cross from life into another life
and never know and still be on my way

# who is playing that drum?

### from 2018

## if I could shift into any shape

I would not have one
I would be the shapeless wind
shaping water, grass, deserts, leaves
I would be breathed
and released, breathed and released
I would be bone hollow and hidden cave
storm and stillness before the storm
I would know the shape of everything

## which shape is real?

in the woods on full moon nights
who can tell? the light has a shape,
the dark has a shape, both solid
as any daylight thing. could you
scrape your shin on that light?
could that darkness grab you
from behind? do you dare
to encounter either one? and what
of your shape, real as a false step,
a broken twig, a stubbed toe.

## dream

planets are mortal
the Earth terminally ill
having contracted
a fatal case of humans
the final stage, my friend weeps

## a still beating heart

is the heart still or beating
beating still, shifting its shape
with every pound of its
tidal drum? sometimes I do not want

to hear my husband's heart
because I know someday it will stop.
sometimes I do not like the roar
of my heart in my ears.

slow down, slow down, still
beating heart. I am listening
to the silence between the beats,
but who, who is playing that drum?

# beyond the world we see

## from 2019

## no footprints

I wish I could leave no footprint
not just a minimal carbon footprint
no footprint in the snow
no footprint in the melting ice flow
at bottom of the field
where the formation of ridges
rivers, mountains, lakes
is laid out in miniature
is happening in slow/fast motion
before my eyes.

I take a few steps, a clumsy bigfoot,
into the slush, such outsized, disproportionate
prints. I retreat.
I will not interfere
I will not mar one more creation
of a world.

## why we love birds

they go where we can never go,
airplanes are not what we mean
when we long for wings.

maybe hang-gliding is close,
I don't know, I've never tried it,
falling that turns into flight.

there are as many kinds of flight as birds,
scissoring swallows, floating raptors,
geese and ravens who talk as they go.

and the starlings who rise as one
and disappear in their spiral turns,
the sky butter to their slicing wings.

and the doves who soften the air
with their sonorous call, and all
the hidden songbirds' songs and seagulls' cries,

cutting through the surf. how
can we not love birds who teach
us sky and cliff and wave?

without them on earth there would
be only noise, noise and no dreams
of the world beyond the world we see.

# dream

cast off mistresses
make themselves terrifying
sunken eyes, warts, rags
they confront the younger ones
warning, welcome, sisterhood

# who does not come to ruin villanelle

who does not come to ruin in the end
if we chance to live long enough we know
we will become the ones whom others tend

like a river we may go round the bend
lay down the hoe, it's been too tough a row
who does not come to ruin in the end

what relief, there's nothing left to defend
let the grass go, it's grown too long to mow
we will become the ones whom others tend

now it's time for us ruthlessly to rend
the dry seed husk of what we've reaped and sow
who does not come to ruin in the end

our torn hearts have eternity to mend
breath will bear us out on its unseen flow
we have become the ones whom others tend

green grass, bright sparks are messages we send
all that rises falls to the sweet below
who does not come to ruin in the end
leave tenderness behind for those who tend

## mermaid

of course I wanted to be a mermaid,
so many little girls do.
there was no Disney in my youth
only Hans Christian Anderson.

I would not have given up
my fishtail for any stupid prince.
as for an immortal soul, who needs one
when you can spend eternity as sea foam?

so forget every version of that story.
there are coral castles to explore
and gardens of exotic blooms
starlight and moonlight filtering

down into the depths and now
and then dawn on the rocks
seabirds and wind and breaking waves
ships to wreck. let the men

come to us, let there be a story
of how the best and truest lover
can earn his tail and grow
gills alongside lungs. who would

not want to breathe and swim
ride currents without fear
dare storms and tidal waves and finally
be seafoam, part sea, part salty air?

# if animals could cook
## after Beatrix Potter

they would first dress up in Edwardian garb
and make tidy homes among the roots
with dried herbs hanging from the rafters
there would be an open hearth, tall enough
to stand in and a cauldron hung over a fire
always merrily blazing. vegetables stolen
from a human garden would be standard fare
for rabbits and there would always be chamomile tea
to sooth a bunny's tummy after close encounters
with a garden hoe or rake.

it is less appealing to consider what cats
might cook, but we know their kitchens
would be decorated with mouse and rat tails,
though rats sometimes turn the dining tables.
rats like their food wrapped in pastry dough.

and toads apparently have a liking for honey
whether by itself or as a sweetener I am not sure.
canine cuisine does not bear thinking about
so I will stop this poem here.

## blessed are

blessed are the bees fastened to the sunflower
blessed are the squirrels scrabbling for nuts
blessed are the monarch butterflies and the milkweed
blessed the still mornings after the traffic subsides

blessed are all children longing for their parents
blessed all parents aching for their children
blessed are those who take one step after another
blessed are those who fall

blessed are the bewildered
blessed are those who bend to pick up trash
blessed are those who make breakfast
blessed are those who can't get up at all

those who mourn must always be blessed
blessed those with the courage not to turn away
blessed are those who share what they have
blessed the earth spinning round with unassuming grace

blessed are those who cry for help
blessed are those who answer, angel, deity, dog or cat
blessed are the birds who show us the sky
blessed the hidden ones who sing

## where I am from

I am from my mother's body
my father's begetting is not an address

I am from my comfortable bed
I am from my cleaned up mess

I am from my deepest despair
I am from the more that is less

I am from nights of dreaming
I am from my second guess

I am from debilitating faith and doubt
I am from the turning on a dime to yes

## harvesting words

we do not live by bread alone,
he said, but by every word
that proceeds from the mouth of god.

I have never seen god's mouth
unless it is the mouth of a river
or a cave or maybe the mouth
of a baby rooting for a breast.

and what is a word? something spoken
or written, bitter or sweet
withering or comforting.
where does a word go when it's done
if it is not something you eat?

I have lived by and for words
they have given and consumed my life,
but I live by them

and the beautiful rare moments
when they cease.

# a planet to adore

from 2020

## prayer as remembering

I remember
we are as connected as tree roots, all fed by the same earth
but we forget

I remember
just a little when I pray each day
what I forget

I remember
all the names I can remember
pray twice for the ones I forget

I remember
so many horrors overheard, heard over and over
I wish I could forget

I remember
I pray in litanies of lists
I pray not to forget

## attempted sonnet

a sonnet must a metaphor extend
the poet then must pick a theme with care
for to this purpose all the lines shall bend
line four already! let me take the dare:
I want to hope again though all seems lost
trees burn, ice melts and species disappear
while billionaires refuse to count the cost
and millions live their lives in desperate fear.
are we at flood tide or our lowest ebb?
I hold my breath and listen for the pause.
the only rhyme available is web
will we make mending it our dearest cause?
at sonnet's end, no guiding metaphor
and yet there's still a planet to adore.

## what does time look like

shadows reaching then shrinking, elongated, squat
sun rising, sun setting, same with the moon
sunrise traveling south then north along the ridge

baby turning into a child, kitten to cat,
the rings in the trunk of a tree
the first age lines on my child's face

the softness of worn clothes
the hole too big to be patched
compost composting

the dead leaves, the new snowdrops
the slowed step, the bent back,
the refurbished nests, the baby birds

the scars in an old tree, the stars
coming out one, then another and another
water turning into steam, hard dry beans now tender

## …someday I'll take it

at the dark of the moon, stars border tree branches
in slippers I stand and look from wooden back steps
the night sky is a vast dare, someday I'll take it

## the fourth morning after the fall of the great oak

I don't know when I'll stop counting
not this first week.
will the tree spirit travel through Bardos
for forty-nine days?

the tree is not a Buddhist
it is a tree, a tree that might
awaken a Buddha
that might awaken me,

that I used to awake to see.
don't look away, I said to my heart
today or my heart said to me.
don't brace against sorrow, surrender.

I was attached to the tree
of course I was, and so I suffer
not gladly but willfully, sturdily
as if my sorrow could stand,

does stand with me every
day in the posture called
embracing the tree when I pray
beside the great fallen white oak.

## the seventh morning

whatever god is may have rested,
on this day. are you resting now?
what is it like to be you on
the seventh day from your falling?
are your roots still seeking
to send food to your branches?
are you wondering what happened
to the light your new baby
leaves were meant to take in?
do you feel the feet of squirrels
and chipmunks as they explore,
reconfiguring their homes in your hollows?

some people called you grandmother
some grandfather, he, she. they wanted
you to be a person. you were, you are
an arboreal being. no pronoun is adequate
for you, so I keep saying tree,
oak, great white oak, tree, beloved tree
fallen tree, hollowed, hallowed tree.
however you know yourself I am with you,
sorrow doesn't rest on the seventh day.

## dream

the tree is falling
the oak tree, the newly green
branches against sky,
blue sky, falling and falling
I can only surrender

## garden

the earth is a garden,
given the chance it grows
it grows back, flowers,
berries, nuts, fruit,
pollen, nectar, beauty,
over and under the sea,
deserts, mountains, swamps.
the earth will flower
the earth wants to feed us, we
didn't ever have to leave
the garden, we don't ever
have to leave.

## peace chant
*set to music by Ruth Cunningham*

peace in each breath
peace in my heartbeat
peace in my kind hands
peace in my rooted feet.

peace at the bounds of my body's light
peace where my soul meets the starry night.

# kneeling

knees are made to bend
so we can squat
beside a small child,
beside a cook fire.
so we can sit in a chair
or on the ground.
their motion is the way
we get up or down.

I used to hate kneeling
in church. what does that say
about god?

I will kneel
to scrub a stubborn stain
from the floor,
to pull weeds, to bring
my forehead to the
earth.

athletes have been chastised
for taking a knee
instead of standing
for the national anthem.
the land is not free
it is bloodstained
owned and exploited by the few.

a planet to adore

a man puts his knee
on another's man's neck
until he dies of asphyxiation.
a few of his brethren
take the knee in a few
scattered cities
while brutality goes on.

now I want to kneel
I want us all to kneel
I want the grass to stain us
instead of blood.

# dear Jesus

dear Jesus, they've hijacked your religion.
*you may recall, I never founded one.*
that is no excuse for what has been done in your name.
*I agree.*
I want you to hurry up and return, overthrow the tyrants.
*you may recall, I did not make much headway with the Roman empire.*
I do recall, the Temple was razed, your people scattered.
*and I was dead already.*
but you keep coming back, or people keep reviving you
*for better and for worse.*
if you are not god,
*which I never claimed to be,*
you became a god.
*so it would seem.*
do you have any power?
*do you?*
not fair.
*I agree.*
how did you feel when you saw the would-be American emperor incite violence to cross a street to wave a bible in front of your church?
*how do you think I felt, choking on tear gas? hit by rubber bullets?*
you were there?
*where else would I be?*
can't you smite him and his minions? they are hurting people, hurting the earth.

# a planet to adore

*why do the innocent suffer? why do the wicked prosper? Job's question.* never answered.
*answered. where were you when I laid the foundations of the earth?* not an answer to injustice.
*I agree.*
Jesus, the very stones are crying out! the rivers, the leviathans. we need help, all my relations need help! if it is left up to humans alone, to the goodness of our hearts, we are doomed. please don't say you agree.
*all right. how's this? heaven on earth is within you, between you, below you, above you, all around you. now.*
don't give me metaphysical bullshit. we need to be saved from ourselves. now!
*I agree.*

# dream

the doctor calls me
terminal diagnosis
death by dinosaur
detected in my bloodwork
brontosaurus and T-Rex

# dream

who is the killer?
who is the one being killed?
do they change places?
I don't know which one I am
I want to stop the murder

# haibun: walking between worlds and times

It sometimes happens when I walk alone, when I don't know where a trail leads, the worlds slip past each other, not quite separate. I am in both, or leaving one for the other. The same thing happens to time. I am all the ages I have ever been, exploring. The earth is all ages, even if I can only catch glimmerings. Just around the corner, I will be in the other world, inside another story. The ancient trees are already there, wind-twisted, lightning hollowed, roots intricate and vast. They know all the things I only guess. Right now they are sinking into their deep winter dream. An aging child walks by, just grazing the surface.

someday I will stay
in this place I keep finding
I won't be sent back

# becoming where I am

## from 2021

## haibun: moving wood

I've been doing it for a couple a months, loading armfuls of wood into a battered wheelbarrow, bringing them into the garage, stacking them according to size, the pile never neat, because of the logs' curving shape. For a moment, in the dim light of the shed, I stop. I am holding in my arms the curving branches I used to trace with my eyes, looking out the window from my bed, by night, by day for seven years. I am holding my tree in my arms. I am holding my tree.

from hollow to bark
how many rings of mourning
I have just begun

# the Buddha finally gets to me

one wing transcending
one wing embracing
suffering

I didn't know
there were two wings

maybe I will
learn to fly

is nonattachment
simply letting go of judgment?

I still don't get enlightenment
I am awake, the Buddha said

I am a dreamer, I answer
I like to take flight
in the dark

## family history in snow

*blizzard of 1888*

My grandmother was just over two months old
when the March blizzard of 1888 shut down the east coast.
Her mother was a country doctor in Connecticut
disinherited for studying with the Blackwell sisters.
Dr. Reid and Aunt Julia had adopted two little girls,
my grandmother, the younger one, a babe in arms.
Best not go home tonight, my great grandmother
said to the wet nurse, just before the white hurricane
struck, sustained winds of forty-five miles an hour,
drifts as high as fifty feet. Did the people around
her sense the magnitude of the coming storm,
despite the mild spring-like day that went before?
Did the animals? Did she? She heeded whatever
warned her and my grandmother lived
who might have starved if she had not.

*when winter was winter*

I believe it is true, winter was winter
when I was young. Of course, I didn't have to
shovel or drive; it was a boon to miss school.
Winter was winter all winter long.
There was no salt or grit in the rectory driveway,
just pure packed snow, and all the kids
came with their flexible flyers to
glide round its curving slope.
We had afternoons with our father in winter,
because one thing my mother did not do
was snow and cold. So he pulled the toboggan
back uphill at the golf course
and rode it down or gave us
a spinning send off in our round flying saucers.

Who knew he could be fun—and safe—
on the cold, fast danger of a snowy slope.

*scientific observation*

I must have been in eighth grade.
We'd moved from the rectory
to North Tower Hill, across a dirt road
from fields where black angus cows
grazed all summer; in winter the fields
belonged to snow. My brother and I
waded out after one storm, our dog
no doubt bounding around us
imperiling the scientific record
I was making for school, measuring
the depths of drifts, noting
their patterns around rocks and posts,
piled on one side, hollowed on the other.
That is, my brother measured, careful, precise.
I recorded the results, not only in my notebook
but in the memory I still keep
of my brother's kind competence
and the bright, drifting steppes of snow.

*my mother is happy*

It must have been when some of us
were teens, returned for vacation from schools
we'd been sent to because she thought
it was necessary or would be good for us.
It's Christmas Eve, and we are snowed in.
No church services, nowhere to go.
No one can go, none of her children
can leave (perhaps never to return
as she always feared whenever we were gone).
I was so happy that night, she tells me later,
all my children together, everyone safe.

becoming where I am

It is not the snowstorm I remember,
it is my mother's confession, of happiness.

*I don't remember*

Surely I played with my children in the snow
took them tobogganing, showed them how to make
snow angels, built snow men and women,
fetched carrots for the nose. Surely. I almost remember
clearing snow from the icy pond for skating,
making tracks, running and sliding, falling down laughing.
Surely the memories are there somewhere,
in their bodies, in mine, but I don't remember
just one time, or another, no snow tableau in a globe
I can turn upside and watch as the snow falls
slowly again and again.

dream

from an old deep well
my daughter draws up my tears
what will they water?

tanka

each prayer is a seed
it knows what to grow into
even if you don't
plant prayers deep where you can't see
earth, rain, light will do the rest

becoming where I am

## suddenly

yesterday for no reason I know
I became aware of my body
and wished it had never been breached
in any way ever
by any man and maybe not even
by childbirth
(though I would never change
one hair on my children's head).
an odd, unprecedented thought
to want to take back all the generous,
torturous access I've given.
when for years I longed
for nothing more than to be
that way between worlds.

how can I wish now to be sealed
impenetrable, shining, whole
protected and complete as a seed?

# old people's fairytale

I am an aging princess wide awake,
watching the vines and briars tangle around me.
the aged prince is here with me
growing vegetables, gazing into his own twilight.
weeds grow wilder, thickets thicker,
no one is seeking us, maybe
one day we will just disappear.

# snapping turtle

has a rock lifted from the water?
I stand and gaze into the pond,
the algae covered rock is the head
of a huge snapping turtle, the same
color as the pond, green, dark, now
seen, now gone, deeper into mud.
I stand still, the rocky head rises
turns, revealing tiny eyes, nose
that breathes the same air as me,
mouth that moments ago nibbled
at the pond weed that clings
to the head I mistook for a rock.
maybe a turtle is kin to rock and
algae and water and mud. maybe
I am kin to everything too, sky
and ground, gnats and mosquitoes
hovering outside my netting.
I just don't blend in as well,
I don't know how to become
where I am.

becoming where I am

## what I hear

when you can't pray
don't

this not praying is a prayer
reach out if you can

if you touch only air
let the wind hold your hand

## snake

I promised you a poem.
twice I have come upon you
crossing the road near my driveway
to the swampy thickets on the other side.

I get out of my car
to encourage you, to motivate
you to move faster while
I stand guard, ready to stop

any cars that come along,
careless cars that drive too
fast on winding roads, with
S curves, the same S curves

in your beautiful spine,
its many vertebrae
echoed in patterns of faint grey
along your black back,

your long and winding road
of a back. you move in
curves. I wish I could just
stand and admire your

graceful, unhurried precision.
go on, I urge you, you're almost there.
I watch you disappear into the dense
dark green, safe and secret again.

## morning prayer

morning is prayer, all I have to do is be there. Hickory nuts drop, birds' wings whir, squirrels chirr, leaves catch light, make shadows as they fall. In the distance, traffic. If I don't judge any of it, if I don't judge myself, I become part of it all. There are conversations I can't hear with my ears going on under my feet. There are stars I can't see, hidden by sunlight. They may be singing as they follow their paths, leaving wakes of shining dust. I don't know. I only know, if I show up, I am here, welcome to morning prayer.

## I wonder

I step out into the cold dawn
I wonder if souls feel cold.
what is it like
to step outside the shelter
of the body?

## beaver

almost dusk, stillness
I hear a sound on the other side
of the beaver pond
with its open water, bounded by lily pads,
dark island humps of mud and sticks.
the sound is not a woodpecker,
quieter, subtler, is that…?
a beaver rises from the water
dark and round, shaped like a lodge
with a back like the grassy hummock
where she is having a quiet snack.
and then she's back in the water,
swimming it silver
before she disappears.

## black bear

We're alone on the long avenue
in the gloaming, you a dark
distinctive shape, me a human
with what I call safety
on the far side of you
and swamp to right and left.

What shall we make of each other?
I sing "by yon bonnie banks
and by yon bonnie braes,"
a song I imagine, for some
unknown reason, bears like.
You seem to listen before

you amble off the trail
to the left. I walk and sing on.
you appear again before me,
closer this time. I sing:
"my life flows on in endless song
how can I keep from singing?"

You lope (your motion so
different from a dog's or
any other being) towards
the parking lot, turning right
just before you reach it,
maybe finding firmer ground.

O bear, bear, bear, bear, yes,
I am afraid but more
I am in love with you,
your ridge-shaped blackness,
the intimate moment we shared
alone together at dusk.

## haibun: what makes us human?

Other animals also love and mourn. many of them build and weave. They sing. they speak. some collect bright shining things. only humans, and not all humans, stand in opposition to the earth, saying, it shall be according to my will, not yours. Is it because we have opposing thumbs that we oppose so much, impose so much? Can we choose to step back into the ebb and flow, the wax and wane, the rise and fall of all that is? How long will we have any choice as we are overtaken by fire, flood, and wind?

such a long, short time
when will we be human/kind?
have mercy on us

# coming in and going out

### from 2022

## thank you, fox

for letting me see you
the graceful, leisurely streak of you
nose to tail, black, russet, silver-tipped
trotting not too fast or slow
leaving your petaled paw prints
in the snow

# eagle message

maybe there is no other meaning than you,
your strength and beauty, your own purpose
as you circle the wild, white water of the creek.

are you hunting for fish, riding currents of air
raised by the meeting of cold waters and warming light?
could you possibly care that I am there?

I think not, but maybe my seeing you
still carries a message for me, some say:
spring, rebirth; others, meeting a challenge

all peoples of the earth tell stories of you.
what can I say? you make me think of the brave ones
in Ukraine. you fill me with longing to be brave.

how often is a choice so clear, as the one embraced
by Volodymyr, for a moment all ambiguity gone?
he risks death to protect his people, his country, that is all.

I pray for such courage and unclouded sight.
risking death has not yet been asked of me
I am challenged to a different kind of fight.

## 23rd psalm assignment: rewrite

you are my shepherd
you take care of me
leading me through the green world
to clear water
you restore my soul
you guide me in the way of truthfulness
for your sake, for mine
when I walk through the shadow
of the valley of death
I am not afraid
you are with me, you comfort me
you prepare a table in the presence
of my enemies, and I share
the feast with them
goodness and mercy follow me
as I follow you
wherever you are is my
dwelling place

## dream

we're renting a truck
to fetch my son from prison,
my daughter and I,
no, don't rent from Enterprise
rent from the revolution

## grandmother

At the ancestor feast, almost everyone tells a story about a grandmother, including me. These words come to me: a grandmother is a portal to the ancestors. Then sorrow comes. I may never be a grandmother. There is still a "may" in front of never, but the word is wavering, a twilight fading into a night of never. I can almost see my grandchild; sometimes I talk to him. If you come, I say, I will be here for you. I believe we both know it might not happen; I believe we both wish it would. We glimpse each other through the veils of ephemeral possibility. What does it mean to be a grandmother with no grandchild? There are trees I call granny, old, wise maples, wind-twisted by the seasons, still putting forth and letting go of leaves. Maybe I will be a granny like that, standing at the edge of a wood or in the middle of a field. Someone like me, full of longing, might stop in my shelter and be comforted.

## blessed be your coming in and your going out

When I go outside, I remember, I am a sensate mammal, among myriad lifeforms, here between the earth and the sky. Senses open to scent, sound, light, the hardness or yield of ground. Outside is huge, I know nothing and everything at once. I am nothing and everything. I remember I am, or was once, wild. But I can go inside when I need to, for warmth or cool, to get dry, to sleep. Some people can't go outside at will, and some can't go inside at will. To go out, to come in is to be blessed indeed.

# break us open not apart

### from 2023

dream

I drink burnt sage tea
there's more to sage than I thought
holy smoke and drink

# wild card

god is the wild card
the joker in the deck
the fool tripping through the tarot
dancing on the cliff's edge
falling, flying

when we pray
we shuffle the deck
we did not make
the deck we only dream
the cards fly and fall

where they will
the wind blows
where it will
the seed dies and rises
again and again

wild card god, your
hands hold the deck
you deal the hands
you laugh when we think
we have control

play me, make me
as wild as you
disastrous or lucky
spin me loose, let
me fall into grace

## what happens…

…to the soul or souls of a forest or a coral reef? We want to believe our souls live beyond our bodies, we want to believe we will see our beloveds again, including, especially, our cats, our dogs. A tree is a life, a forest is a life for trees, birds, all, manner of mammal, reptile, amphibian, insects, mushrooms, life of the canopy, life of the understory, life of root and hollow. Where does the soul of such a being, such beings go? How do I mourn, how to imagine reunion at my own death with a being my kind killed, knowingly, unknowingly. Arboricide. I know less of coral reefs; I have never seen one, but I know they are the forests of the sea, and they are dying of excess heat. We are all in hot water, we are in hot air. We are walking a burning earth. How do we mourn all we have murdered?

## lament

you whose name is known and unknown
where are you, why have you left us here
at the mercy and mercilessness of one another?

you whose name we claim to know
we have forgotten: we are one, we are the other
you are with us across all closed borders

you are the one we call ally, enemy
you are the one dying in our arms
you are the one holding our brokenness

you whose name we cry out in every tongue
break us open not apart, quiet our clamor,
do not leave our hearts forsaken, heart of our hearts.

## all souls day tanka

I honor all souls
(who can know who is a saint?)
the souls of lost trees
the souls of absconded bees
all souls still clinging to life

## what does prayer do?

it has not brought lasting peace anywhere
yet people pray for peace every day

people have said to me bitterly
prayer does not work, I don't disagree

prayer does not produce measurable results
does not reliably cure the sick

or secure anything we want and still
we pray, for what we think is best

I know less and less each day
about everything, why we are

the way we are as a species, why
we are both kind and cruel

and least of all why anything
we call god would allow such bad behavior

o whirlwind speak to me, scatter me,
chaff or wheat, what does it matter

break us open not apart

## the yard tucked in…

…for winter rest, perennials cut back or skeletal, annuals gone, spring bulbs planted. Leaves moved from the grass to make brown blankets for the gardens. I miss the flowers; I treasure the last leaf colors, barberry, winterberry, bittersweet. I am astonished every year by all massive green life that goes back to the earth. Yet there is a feeling of comfort, like a child, or a very old person, tucked into bed, covers smoothed and warm.

# a setting sun that will rise

## from 2024

### gnaw

in my yard there is coyote scat.
I never cleared it away as I might a dog's.
one night I'd heard the pack right under my window
not howling but yipping, impossibly high and wild.
my cat and I, both awake, sat frozen
which is to say perfectly still, hardly breathing
not exactly frightened but awed
secure in each other's warmth, in the house,
in the bed on the second floor out of reach
of the coyotes on the other side of the wall.

in the field beyond the house
I found their killing ground
where they flattened the grass
as they tore and gnawed, many
scattered turkey feathers, half
a discarded deer leg, bone and hoof.

the scat is still there in the yard,
fading, ashen, like coals grown old and cold,
disappearing into the grass, then down
deeper, turning into earth who
slowly gnaws it all.

## hands of

god has hands, as in, we are in the hands of
god has a potter wheel and handles us as clay
sometime in rage smashing the clay on the wheel
pray there is also kindness in that god's hand

the fates, all three, or however many there are, have hands
they weave with them, and when they must, snip, snip
do they use scissors or just hands to snap
the thread that's done, hands to tie it off

someone's hands knead the opening to the world
catch the baby, pull her from water into air
the mother holds her baby, strokes, with her hand, the cheek
counts the toes, wipes away all the tears

someone's hand holds the hand of the dying one
someone's hands wash the body while still warm
before it cools to clay that can no longer
be worked by anyone's hand, not even god's

## life is nonbinary…

…despite parts of plants and people that might go together to make some more life. Life is a tangle, more than predator and prey, though, yes, life feeds on life to give life. Light and shadow are always shifting, making microclimates wherever they go. Even we messy humans are so much more than good or bad, functional or dys. Polarity may make the molecules and the planets go round, but the dance is so much wilder than we know. Death and breath rhyme for a reason. Eden is still here, around us and within us. Let's stop casting each other out.

# seek ye

seek ye first whatever is heaven
kingdom, queendom, commonwealth
or more likely for me
a garden overgrown, wavering into
wildness; or these words,
rich or poor, the pathways
they make in my despair
the way water furrows
new ways though the meadow
after rain

o if I seek heaven first
will my chores get done
will all my loves be loved
will all else be added unto me
like he said?
and what else is it I keep
blindly seeking, forgetting
heaven is at hand
all around
within

## haibun: my mother's handwriting…

…on an index card. How did her recipe for Irish Soda Bread—and her not Irish and her not someone who liked to bake from scratch—find its way into my tattered Moosewood cookbook among the salads, multi-bean the one I've looked up. And if it has been there a long time (a long time, before her death 27 years ago?) how have I never noticed it? Her printing small, neat and distinctive, slanting to the left, as no one else's does. I can hear her, see her writing for me, her note that Betty uses baking powder instead of soda, her admonition not to forget the raisins, though she forgot to tell me when to fold them in. Me, she wrote this for me. I must have followed her instructions at least once, maybe more. Maybe I will follow them again someday. Maybe I will just gaze at her handwriting, there in the only cookbook I use with any frequency, tucked into the crease, springing out at me, bringing her back, her thoroughness, a crease of concentration on her forehead, her frowning precision, this gift from someone who didn't love to cook to a daughter more like her than either of us ever knew.

handed down to me
this handwritten recipe
living memory

## shy joy

joy has been waiting,
under some wing
or perched in a tree,
for the noise to stop

then joy drifts down quietly,
think of cottonwood seeds
think of mist lingering
till it turns to light

joy has been waiting,
a cluster of purple iris
almost hidden in the deep meadow.
waiting for me to see.

## free to go or stay

here is a good trick
if you are not free to go
make the choice to stay

## who gives us freedom

sometimes in love songs
the true lover sets
the beloved free

sometimes parents
grant their children freedom
long after they are gone

sometimes children
free themselves from their parents
long after they've let go

freedom is give and take
wings spread then folded again
a setting sun that will rise

## dream

sex with a sperm whale?
the minister and I joke
divine perspective

# black white red

fairytale colors

black as night
as bottomless sea
as the pupil of an eye

as death

white as snow
as moon
as milk

as death

red as blood
as berries
as cardinals in a thicket

as death

a child's joke: black and white and re(a)d all over

the colors a priestess wears
when she puts on her  power

life
death
rebirth

## grandchild speaks

I am waiting
playing with pebbles on the shore
so many colors here
here I can dive into waves
and breathe water like air

I see you missing me
I would come to you if I could
I'm not afraid, the waves
go up and down, but they
don't carry me to your shore

there are other children here
who remember being old once
who remember time
before it never stopped
I miss you too, grandmother

## Lughnasadh

the sun is going into the dark
into the grain, into the ground
into the oven, into the mouth,
into the belly, where it will
burn, burn into bone and flesh

what is my harvest, what is my grief
what is this fierceness of life
burning, burning in bone and flesh
now I am singing, now I am silent
words going into the dark are enough

# heron

I'm the only human here
standing by the water
on the soft hemlock needles
(where my footfall made no sound)
standing as still as I can
to watch the heron whose
stillness surpasses the still dead
wood rising from the swamp,
the heron the same color
as the wood, as stone, as sky
where the clouds stand still too.

a smaller darker bird,
maybe a red egret, sits still
on a nearby log. do we share
stillness or is mine
an irrelevant reverence?

then the heron stretches out
her neck, (or his, who knows?)
when she retracts, it pulls
her soundless, high-stepping
feet forward, once, twice.
then her long bill dives
and rises with something
alive, a frog, a fish, I am too
far away to know but not
too far to watch her catch
disappear and make its way
--still alive?—down her long,
long throat.

a setting sun that will rise

when her meal is in her belly
she stretches her neck, her beak
to the sky, gives a scratchy
guttural cry and half flies
half leaps over lily pads
to a light again a small distance away.

the egret on the log hasn't moved
neither have I; the stillness still
not done with me.

## what if I could change the setting

of our lives, back to when the attic
still held hundreds of unsorted years

and the ancestors leavings remained
in boxes, mouse droppings and dust.

would it be better than the too-quick
sorting, the hasty, heartrending

decisions I will second-guess
regret, even repent? the last of

our line helped not only hauling
but witnessing, discerning.

how much to leave to them to sort
when we are gone? I hope just enough.

ancestors, we stirred up your dusts
the mystery of your memories. now

we can't reset our lives to mere
days before. we honored you

and begged your pardon, lit candles,
in our own fashion, prayed, and I

sacrificed my own memories and
papers even more thoroughly than

a setting sun that will rise

yours. I can't turn the time back,
I won't be sorting through the dumpster.

rest in peace, wherever, whatever
you are now. if nothing else, know this:

you can be proud of the youngest
of this line, even if they are the last.

# travelling communion

In a little black case, in my family for more than a hundred years, the host, the wine, the chalice, carried to the shut in, the sick, the dying. There were three and a half wafers left and wine long since vinegar. My children suggested I take the body and blood of Christ, place it and pour it outside. I went to the great fallen oak and took communion with my ancestors, dipping the half wafer in the wine, then pouring the wine on the earth and placing the last three wafers in the hollow of the oak.

When she found out what I had ingested, my daughter shrieked with horror. She looked up how long wine and wafers can be kept (18 months for wafers, wine less). Not more than thirty years! I was not concerned. My children don't know firsthand how dry and strangely lifeless those wafers are even when fresh. They can't go stale. And, I kept saying, I only dipped, not sipped. I was not worried. I was glad for this communion with my ancestors and the earth.

a setting sun that will rise

## the priesthood of the transfer station

cheerful people, ready to help,
ready to answer any question
as we confess our waste.
all that we've used, used up, or can't use
they accept and direct without judgment.

journal pages and junk mail
to be made into toilet or other paper
uncountable cans of seltzer
glass bottles with their loud slide into the bin
the black bags full of unrecyclable sin
a two dollar penance for each.
we live in a commonwealth of waste, impoverishing
our planet, the transfer station is a holy place.

I leave feeling (temporarily)
absolved, lightened, renewed in my faltering faith.
it is impossible to sin no more
we will be back next weekend.

# my ghosts

when the sun rises over the ridge
I turn from its blinding brilliance.
there is my shadow at its longest,
flowing over the ground, the gardens, the trees.

do I speak aloud? I am not sure.
I hear myself say, oh it's you.
you'll still be here, when I am gone,
and I know it's true.

shadow or ghost, seen, unseen,
some part of me will remain
in this yard, as some part of me
is still standing on a tidal island

breathing the scent of salt
and roses. you don't have to be dead
to be a ghost, only gone,
leaving your love behind.

## Ania's wisdom

"of everything," she says "the garden
teaches me the most about life."

we plant, tend and intend, but the plants
go where they will, thrive
or fail according to reasons
we sometimes guess and sometimes
cannot fathom.
logic and miracle
coexist, grace is your mistakes
being overgrown.

# companions on the way

## from 2025

## companions

when I go back to the place
that is the love of my life
I greet all the trees, and then
cross the gap in the wall
to follow the path in the field
my feet made.
the fox still follows the path.
I see light footprints
atop the glazed snow,
the fox follows the path
as far as it goes.

I have seen the fox
the fox has seen me.
mostly we have seen
each other's footprints.
so comforting to know
in this way, we are still
companions on the way.

## walking in the rain

when I walk outside in serious rain
I feel like I am seeing the real world
the secret world, the one that does not
retreat from weather, the world

of water pouring off leaves, dampening
bark, pooling in ditches, the world
of veils and sheets of rain, of birds
in thickets, roots reaching for a drink.

I don't know if I am welcomed,
noticed or not, but I feel like a
VIP with a pass backstage
where the real magic is made.

# the way I find (momentary) peace

walking alone, anywhere, any weather,
a frost crystal floating in the air
a hedge of shining forsythia
even a muddy ditch
empty chairs set out by a pond
whatever I notice when I walk.

in town the neat or messy yards,
one street with a wooden goose on each porch,
tended or neglected gardens, small birds in thickets.

it's the noticing, not always of beauty.
it is being at liberty to notice
sight, sound, scent, the bells every half hour,
the down-shifting trucks,
whiffs of diesel or damp earth,
alarmed and alarming squawks of geese,
air wild or still, warm or cold, dry or damp.
how my senses, alert, carry me
beyond myself, remind me
there's a world going on, even now,
no matter what.

## aging youth

it is sometimes hard
to look at how my generation
has aged, maybe especially those
who turn up at rallies.

a scruffy looking bunch, I'd say.
paunches, extra chins, scraggly hair,
baggy clothes, no fashion sense
something I like about myself

till I see it en masse. once
we were as adorable
as any younger ones, all
downy and shiny.

did my parents' generation
age with more dignity and formality
or did they also cling to an appearance
youthful in their day?

# if something gives you joy...

...say thank you
do not maunder on
about unworthiness
undeserving.

of course you do not
deserve good fortune
anymore than anyone
deserves ill fortune.

dessert is something sweet
to be savored.

cause and effect are real
but grace is always amazing.
there is no accountant
in the sky or under the earth,
just a tangled weave
too brilliant for you to see.

justice is something you must
love and labor for,
just because.

when injustice prevails
do not beat your breast.
just stand, like all living things
grass and trees, even if
you are laid low
or broken.

you don't deserve to suffer
either.

## childbed

an archaic term for childbirth
"she was brought to bed of a son," an archaic way
of saying she gave birth to a boy.

not all babies are born in a bed
there are women who squat in the fields
and then go back to work.

but the old word reminds us
birth, begetting, and dying do happen
(though not always) in bed, ground

for life arising and returning.
we went to bed together, such
an evocative term for coupling,

the vertical going horizontal
trees falling to the forest bed
becoming a bed for lichen and fern.

all seeds need a bed, all animals,
deep dens, long grass where deer
leave the impression of their fleet bodies,

birds and squirrels build beds in trees
there are clam beds and beds of seaweed
and sand beds where turtles bury eggs.

if we could, maybe we'd bed down
in clouds or nestle among galaxies
or, like cats, find a bed in a patch of sun.

may we be brought to bed
of our truest selves, our sweetest dreams
may our beds be soft after a hard day, a hard life.

## where does it go?

when memory leaves someone
where does it go? I have memorized
what I can of his life
but that is my memory.

the wind blows
the clouds gather or disperse
the rain falls, what does not
return to the air
goes underground.

## vultures

I look up the oracular meaning of many vultures
patience, protection, purity, beginning again.

I've already googled the natural cause, there's an updraft,
a vulture elevator to the thermals, they cruise

round and round, over the parking lot, then
up HW Dubois Drive, all the way to the rising moon.

they are not just circling for death, their circle
is the circle of life, death and winged rebirth.

if it were legal I would like to bequeath them
my dead body. what death can I offer now?

would dead hopes feed you, the dead and gone
parts of my life, do dead dreams nourish?

if I relinquish them, will the updraft carry me
to a vulture's eye view of life and death?

## tender

the newly bare ground is soft,
yielding as flesh, it is flesh,
so much life under brown grass.
this tender earth, muddy, frozen
or parched, with rocks outcropping
and rivers low or flooding
gives us everything, is everything,
let's walk tenderly, remembering.

www.ingramcontent.com/pod-product-compliance
Lightning Source LLC
Chambersburg PA
CBHW061800070526
44586CB00023B/2649